EVERYDAY SCIENCE

Making Waves:

Sound

Steve Parker

Heinemann
LIBRARY
Chicago, Illinois

For information, address the publisher:
Heinemann Library, 100 N. LaSalle, Suite 1200, Chicago, IL 60602
Customer Service: 888-363-4266
Visit our website at www.heinemannlibrary.com

Printed and bound in China by South China Printing Company.
08 07 06 05 04
10 9 8 7 6 5 4 3 2 1

Library of Congress Cataloging-in-Publication Data
Parker, Steve.
  Making waves : sound / Steve Parker.
     p. cm. -- (Everyday science)
Summary: An overview of sound, describing what it is and how it is
formed and used and discussing properties associated with sound, such
as pitch, volume, and speed.
Includes bibliographical references and index.
  ISBN 1-4034-4814-0 (HC), 1-4034-6420-0 (PB)
 1. Sound--Juvenile literature. [1. Sound.] I. Title. II. Everyday
science (Heinemann Library (Firm))
  QC225.5.P35 2004
  534--dc22

                              2003014788

Acknowledgments
The publishers would like to thank the following for permission to reproduce photographs:
Corbis pp.7, **22**, **42**, **52**; Getty pp.**4**, **49**; Greenhill Photo pp.**19**, **26**, Greenhill Photo/Mayers
p.**5**; Harcourt Index p.**12**; Kris Krogh p.**37**; OSF/Okapia/Staebler p.**28**, OSF/Howard Hall p.**32**;
Patrick Ford p.**27**; Redferns/Hutson p.**30**,Redferns/Resource Photo p.**35**, Redferns/Gibbons
p.**45**, Redferns p.**46**, Redferns Sims p.**47**; Rex Features p.**51**; SPL/Motta p.**21**, SPL/Deep Light
Productions p.**24**, SPL/Watts p.**36**, SPL/Syred p.**48**; Trip p. **39**.
Cover photograph of the audience at an open-air concert reproduced by permission of Getty
Images/Stone. Artwork by Ascenders pp.**6**, **8**, **13**; David Woodroffe p.**41**; Jeff Edwards p.**20**;
Mark Franklin pp.**10**, **15**, **17**, **29**, **31**, **33**.

The publishers would like to thank Robert Snedden for his assistance in the preparation of this
book.

Contents

Sounds in Our World

We can close our eyes, but we cannot shut our ears. Sounds are all around us, all the time. Even if we are somewhere really quiet, we can still hear the faint hum of machinery, the faraway throb of traffic, or perhaps the whisper of the wind. Even our own bodies make sounds. Our heart beats "thump-thump," and air whooshes gently in and out of our lungs. Some sounds are useful, such as a tone that says we have a phone message, a siren, or a shout of warning. Our sense of hearing is central to our everyday life. Perhaps the only time we are not aware of sounds is when we are asleep. Yet we can be awakened in an instant by a sudden, unfamiliar loud noise.

Sounds like nothing on Earth

Most sounds we hear are made by people, animals, musical instruments, machines, or natural events such as rain and wind. Some sounds, though, are totally artificial. They are created inside electronic devices such as computers and synthesizers. They are patterns of electrical signals and are played through loudspeakers. These electronic sounds can be made so strange they can seem to come from another world.

Sounds so important

Sound is important in all our activities. We talk to people and hear what they say, often without a moment's thought. We hear lessons at school and chatter with our friends. Someone's mood can be expressed by a small sound, such as a "tsk tsk" or a sigh. A few spoken words can affect our whole lives by telling about a terrible tragedy, bringing comfort, or spreading happiness.

Personal sound
Earphones are designed for private listening so that others cannot hear.

Sound is also a huge part of our leisure time and enjoyment. We listen to voices, music, and sound effects on the radio and television, in the movies, and on personal music systems. We make special outings to hear singers, actors, musicians, and DJs performing live. The latest hits in the music charts can reach millions of people and also earn millions of dollars for recording artists. All of this is based on sound.

Scientific sound

The science of sound is known as acoustics. It is a huge area of scientific research, industrial applications, and business activities. Work with sound takes place in various areas. Some acoustical engineers work to reduce it, for instance by making cars and planes less noisy. They also study ways to amplify or improve it by designing louder and clearer music systems. Some study ways to help people with hearing problems. Some sounds can be almost unnoticed, such as background music in elevators, stores, and shopping centers. The work behind these sounds involves many technologies and machines, including microphones, loudspeakers, synthesizers, computers, tapes, discs, and recording equipment.

All of these areas need an understanding of sound—what it is, how it is made, how it can be changed, and how it travels, or is propagated. Sounds can be put to use in hundreds of different ways. They can be bounced around; made louder, softer, higher, or lower; recorded and played back; and used to smash objects into bits.

Features of Sound

Sound is a form of energy, just as light, heat, electricity, and motion are all forms of energy. However, sound is a very weak form of energy compared to other forms. If all the sound energy from a cheering crowd at a sporting event were converted into heat energy, there might be just enough to make a few cups of hot coffee. If the same were done with all the light energy from the same event, there would be enough heat energy to make thousands of cups of coffee!

Million million

The difference in energy content between very loud sounds and very quiet ones is huge. The noise of a big truck roaring by contains about one million million times more energy than the sound of a buzzing mosquito. When you hear a sound at a certain volume and then it gets slightly louder, by just enough for you to hear the change, that sound has doubled its energy content.

Sounds on the move

Sound is often spoken of as traveling in waves. It is also pictured as up-and-down waves. However, this picture is not really accurate. Most of the sounds we hear travel through the air to our ears. They travel as regions of high and low air pressure.

Sound waves
When there is no sound, the tiny particles of air are spread evenly. A sound travels as regions of high pressure, where the particles are closer together, alternating with regions of low pressure, where they are farther apart.

low pressure   high pressure   atoms and molecules of air

Air is made up of billions of tiny particles, called atoms and molecules. Atoms and molecules are far too small to see. Nevertheless, these particles carry sound by moving back and forth in the direction that the sound is traveling.

Vibrations and pressure

A sound source, such as a loudspeaker, vibrates. That is, it moves quickly back and forth. As it moves forward, it bumps into the air particles right in front of it. This pushes them closer together, so they form a region of higher air pressure. These crowded air particles push into the next region, which is slightly farther from the loudspeaker, and so on. In this way the region of high air pressure moves away from the loudspeaker.

Low and high

After the loudspeaker has moved forward, it moves backward, as the next part of its back-and-forth vibration. This makes extra space for the air particles right next to it. They move into the space, spreading farther apart as they do so. As a result, the space right next to the speaker is now a region of lower pressure. This area of lower pressure moves forward in the same way as the higher pressure did a split second before.

Very fast vibrations

The next back-and-forth vibration of the speaker creates another region of higher air pressure, followed by lower pressure, and so on. All this happens very fast—the speaker vibrates hundreds or thousands of times per second. The result is sound that travels, or is propagated, as regions of high and low pressure that move through the air. As all this happens, however, the air particles do not move very far. Even for a very loud sound, each particle moves less than 0.02 inch (0.5 mm). The sound travels mainly because each particle bumps into other particles nearby, which do the same.

Sound Waves

Sound travels as movements of atoms and molecules, as described on pages 6–7. A sound wave moving through the air consists of regions of high air pressure, where the air atoms and molecules are closer than normal, and regions of lower pressure, where they are farther apart. A high-pressure region is always followed by a low-pressure region and vice versa.

Scientists call this pattern of movement a longitudinal wave. However, it is difficult to draw such a wave pattern in a quick and simple way. There are too many dots! So sound waves are usually pictured as an up-and-down wavy line. In science, this line is known as a transverse wave. Each region of high pressure of the actual sound wave in air is shown as a peak of the wavy line. A region of low pressure is shown as a trough. For most purposes, this is a helpful way to picture and understand sound waves.

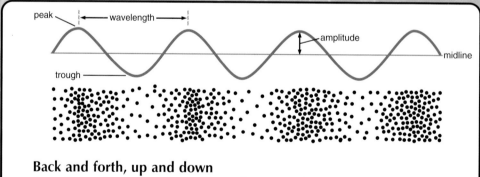

Back and forth, up and down
Sounds travel as movements of particles in air (shown on page 6 and above). However, sounds are usually shown as up-and-down waves, each with a peak that shows where the particles are close together.

Invisible and visible

Sounds moving through air are invisible. The particles of air are so tiny and far apart that our eyes cannot see them. Sounds travel through other substances as well. They can move through liquids, such as water and oil, and solids, such as wood and metal.

Sounds travel through these substances in exactly the same way as through air, as movements of the particles that make up the substance. Sometimes the back-and-forth movements, or vibrations, of an object that makes a sound are big enough to see. A ringing bell, a plucked guitar string, or a beaten drum all move too fast for our eyes to follow each vibration. But we do see the overall movement as a blur.

Silent space

Sounds must have matter to travel through. They cannot travel if there are no particles to carry them. So sounds do not travel through a vacuum, which is a place where there is nothing, not even air. Space is a vacuum. Therefore, sounds cannot travel through it. If you were in space and a rocket blasted straight past you, you would hear nothing. However, other types of waves, such as light and heat, which are very different from sound waves, can travel through a vacuum.

Spreading out

Sounds do not continue for long distances. Otherwise, we would hear the sounds made in faraway places, and the world would be a much noisier place! In air, sounds gradually spread out, or disperse, to cover a bigger and bigger area—just as a light beam spreads out from a flashlight. As the sounds spread out, their energy decreases because it is spread over a greater area—again, like the flashlight beam, which becomes dimmer as it widens.

Fading away

Also, as sound waves travel, their energy is soaked up by the motion of the particles in air. The energy changes into motion energy, and so it decreases. In addition, sounds hit solid objects such as floors, walls, and the ground. These objects soak up some of their energy. For sound, these processes are invisible. But again, we can see a similar process happen with a beam of light, which is blocked by objects in its path. The energy of a sound gradually spreads out, disperses, fades away, and is soaked up into the surroundings.

Loud and Soft Sounds

Sound has three major features. These are volume (loudness), pitch, (from very high to very deep) and speed of travel. In scientific terms, these features are known as intensity, frequency, and velocity of propagation. The diagram of a sound wave is useful for describing these features.

Volume and intensity

Sounds vary in volume. A roar is louder than a whisper. Volume is related to the intensity, or amount of energy, in the sound. In the typical diagram of a sound wave, this is usually represented as the height of the wave, also known as its amplitude. This is the distance between the middle point of the wave and the highest part of the peak, which is usually the same as the distance between the middle point of the wave and the lowest part of the trough. The taller the wave, the louder the sound.

Decibel scale

The usual way to measure a sound's intensity is with the decibel scale. One decibel (dB), is one-tenth of a bel, which is a unit named after Scottish-born American scientist and speech teacher Alexander Graham Bell.

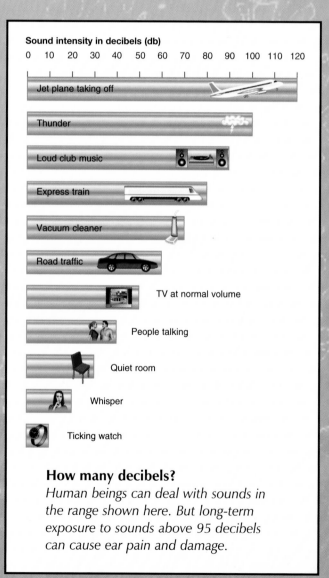

Sound intensity in decibels (db)

0 10 20 30 40 50 60 70 80 90 100 110 120

Jet plane taking off

Thunder

Loud club music

Express train

Vacuum cleaner

Road traffic

TV at normal volume

People talking

Quiet room

Whisper

Ticking watch

How many decibels?
Human beings can deal with sounds in the range shown here. But long-term exposure to sounds above 95 decibels can cause ear pain and damage.

Alexander Graham Bell (1847-1922)

Alexander Graham Bell grew up in Scotland. His father and grandfather were experts on the human voice. They used their knowledge to help deaf people learn to speak clearly. In 1873, Bell became a professor at Boston University. There, he experimented on changing the sound waves that make up the human voice into an electric current. In 1876, he invented a device that could send such an electric current along a wire and change the current back into sound at the other end. This device was the telephone.

The decibel scale measures energy content, which is slightly different from what we hear as loud or quiet with our ears. But intensity and loudness are usually similar enough for the decibel scale to be useful in everyday life.

More means louder

In the decibel scale, the more decibels, the louder the sound. Examples of sounds and their decibel levels are shown in the diagram. The numbers on the decibel scale can be confusing. Every increase of 10 decibels on the scale means the energy has increased 10 times. For example, You might think that a sound of 20 decibels, such as very quiet talking, has twice as much energy as a sound of 10 decibels. But it actually has 10 times as much. A sound of 30 decibels has 100 times, not 3 times, the energy of a 10 decibel sound, and so on.

Adaptable ears

We cannot always trust our ears to judge the true loudness of a sound or compare volumes of different sounds. Electronic devices called decibel-meters (dB-meters), are used to measure sound intensity accurately.

The sensitivity of our ears to sounds varies, depending on the sounds' loudness. If exposed to very loud sounds, the ear adapts to reduce the effect of the loudness and avoid damaging the delicate parts of the inner ear. So ears that are used to high-volume sounds, such as the 90-decibel roar of traffic or very loud music, shut down to protect themselves. In such cases, people probably do not hear normally again until their ears recover. This usually takes several hours. On the other hand, a person who is used to silence hears a sound of 30 to 40 decibels as pretty loud.

Pitch and Frequency

If sounds are represented as up-and-down waves, an important feature is the wavelength. This is the distance from a point on one wave, such as the highest part of the peak, to the same point on the next wave, in this case the highest point of the next wave's peak. The length of a sound wave is related to another feature of sound—its pitch, or frequency. This is the number of complete waves passing a certain place in a given time, usually one second. The frequency, or number of waves passing by, is measured in units called hertz (Hz). These units are named after German scientist Heinrich Hertz (1857–1894), who carried out some of the first experiments with radio waves. A frequency of one hertz is one wave per second.

Ups and downs

Wavelength and frequency depend on each other. If one changes, so does the other. The longer the waves, the fewer of them will pass in one second, compared to shorter waves traveling at the same speed. This means the shorter the wavelength, the higher the frequency, because more waves can pass in one second. (Imagine different vehicles going past front to back, all at the same speed. More short cars would pass in a certain time, compared with long vehicles—that is, short cars would be more frequent than long trucks.)

For sound waves, we hear the result of this as the pitch of the sound. High-frequency sounds

Rumbling roar
The deep, rumbling sound of a huge truck is made up of waves that are several yards or meters long.

Examples of frequencies

human voice	mostly 80–1500 Hz
hissing sounds	up to 4000 Hz
dog's growl	400–700 Hz
cat's meow	700–1500 Hz
bird's song	2000–12,000 Hz
grasshopper's chirp	5000–100,000 Hz
bat's squeak	10,000–150,000 Hz

with short waves have a high pitch. This means that they are shrill and squeaky. Examples are the top notes of a piano or guitar, or the song of a bird. Low-frequency sounds with long waves have a low pitch. They are deep or rumbling. Examples are the boom of thunder, the bass notes of a piano or guitar, or the growl of a large dog.

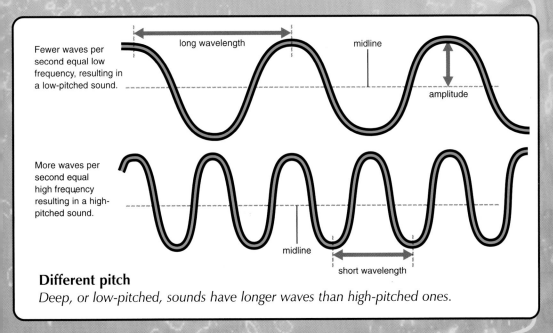

Fewer waves per second equal low frequency, resulting in a low-pitched sound.

long wavelength

midline

amplitude

More waves per second equal high frequency resulting in a high-pitched sound.

midline

short wavelength

Different pitch
Deep, or low-pitched, sounds have longer waves than high-pitched ones.

Lows and highs

How long are sound waves? The musical note known as middle C, in the middle of a piano keyboard, has a wavelength of about 4 feet (1.2 m) and a frequency of 256 hertz. The deep notes of a bass guitar, double-bass, or bass drum have low frequencies, less than 100 hertz. This means that their waves are several yards or meters long. Spoken sounds such as the *s* in *hiss,* and the *t* in *tick-tock,* go up to 4000 hertz, with waves that are just an inch, or a few centimeters long. Sound frequencies range from just a few hertz to hundreds of thousands.

Speed of Sound

Sounds need a substance, or medium, made of particles to travel through. For us, this substance is usually air. Sounds pass through other substances, including liquids such as water, and solids such as metal, wood, and plastic.

Nearer and nearer

Sounds move as particles that bump into each other. However, the tiny particles in a gas, such as air, are fairly far apart and unlikely to bump into each other. So sounds do not travel through air very fast or far. Water molecules are much closer together, so they are more likely to bump into each other. As a result, sounds travel much faster and farther in water. In solids, especially hard, stiff ones, such as metal and glass, particles are even closer together. They are far more likely to bump into their neighbors as they move. So sounds travel even faster and farther in solids such as these.

Fast and slow sounds

The speed of sound in air is usually said to be about 1,115 feet (340 m) per second (760 mph, or 1,220 km/h). This is only partly true. Sound speed varies with the temperature of the air and the distance above Earth.

Air near the ground is denser. This means that it has more particles in a certain volume. Air higher up is thinner, with fewer particles in the same volume. Sounds travel faster in denser air than in thinner air. Temperature affects the speed of sound because it also affects the density of air. So it is better to say that the speed of sound is about 1,115 feet (340 m) per second at sea level and at a temperature of 68°F (20°C). The speed falls gradually to 968 feet (295 m) per second (660 mph, or 1,060 km/h) where the air is very thin, far above Earth.

Faster than sound

Some objects, such as jet planes and rockets, travel through air faster than the speed of sound. This is known as supersonic flight. As they go faster than the speed of sound, they create shock waves, called sonic booms, in the air. A sonic boom can be heard from far away as a low thunderlike thud. The first supersonic plane was the American Bell X-1. It was flown by Chuck Yeager in 1947.

The Mach scale

Because the speed of sound varies so much, it is difficult to compare in different places. For example, a plane with a top speed of 980 feet (300 m) per second could fly faster than sound very high up, but not down near the ground. The Mach scale, named after Ernst Mach, gets around this problem. The speed of sound at a certain time and place is called Mach 1. Twice the speed of sound is Mach 2, and so on.

Ernst Mach (1838-1916)

Ernst Mach was an Austrian physicist and philosopher. He had many scientific interests. He described wave features, such as sound and light. He studied the human eye and ear. And he examined how scientists do experiments and prove their knowledge. In the 1880s, he photographed objects as they traveled faster than sound. His photos revealed the shock waves that formed in the air in front of these fast-moving objects.

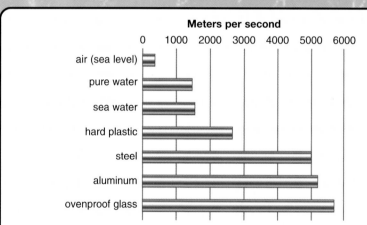

Meters per second

Speeds of sound
Sound's velocity is shown for different substances, or media, in meters per second. In general, the heavier or denser a substance, the faster sound travels through it.

Listen for the train

Sounds travel faster and farther through hard, stiff solids than through air. We can hear this as we wait at a train station. The sound of the approaching train is carried forward by the rails (and then by air a short distance from our ears), as clinking and clanking. We hear this long before we hear the sounds of the train carried only through the air.

The Doppler Effect

Christian Doppler (1803-1853)

Austrian physicist Christian Doppler used math to predict the Doppler effect, the change of a wave's frequency as sender and receiver move relative to each other. He showed this in 1842 using a train, which had been only recently invented. Doppler had a group of trumpeters play a steady note as they traveled in an open train car. A group of musicians on the ground listened to the note. They all agreed that the note became lower in pitch as the train sped past.

Strange things happen to sounds when the source of the sound is moving relative to the person who is hearing it. If the sound source and the listener are standing still in relation to each other, the sound waves travel through the air to the person in the way already described. The person hears the true pitch, or frequency, of the sound. But this is not the case if either the sound source or the listener is moving. Austrian physicist Christian Doppler discovered the reasons why in 1842, and this effect is named after him.

Higher pitch

Imagine that the sound source moves a very short distance toward the listener as it sends out sound waves one after another. After sending out the peak of one sound wave, the source moves a little bit closer to the listener before it sends out the next peak. This means the peak has caught up slightly with the peak in front, and is closer to it than if the sound source stayed still. The same happens with the next wave, and the next. The result is that the peaks of the waves are pressed more closely together than they would be if the sound source was standing still compared to the listener. Closer-together peaks mean shorter waves. This, in turn, means a higher frequency. As a result, the listener hears a sound that is higher in pitch.

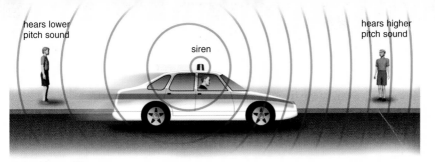

hears lower pitch sound

siren

hears higher pitch sound

Doppler effect

As a sound source moves forward between each wave, the waves are closer together in front, and farther apart behind. The effect is especially noticeable with high-pitched, fast-moving sources, such as police sirens.

Lower pitch

If a sound source is moving away from the listener, the reverse happens. As each sound wave is produced, the source has moved a little farther away. As a result, the peaks of the waves are stretched out as they travel backward toward the listener. Longer waves mean lower frequency. As result, the listener hears a sound that is lower in pitch.

We can hear the Doppler effect especially well when noisy, fast-moving objects go past. For example, race cars, airplanes, and trains all make high-pitched sounds as they approach. Then the sounds fall in pitch as the objects speed past and travel away— "niiiiiiaaaaaaoooooow."

Doppler yourself

The Doppler effect works in exactly the same way if the listener is moving, rather than the sound source. Imagine that you are traveling in a car with the window open. You pass a motorcycle revving its engine by the roadside. The pitch of the motorcycle engine seems to fall as you go by. But it does not really. What you hear is the Doppler effect in action.

The sonic boom

A very loud, sudden example of the Doppler effect is the sonic boom. When an object travels faster than sound, it is moving forward faster than the sound waves it makes. It leaves the sound waves behind itself, and they bunch up and spread out. The effect is like a huge invisible cone trailing along through the air behind the craft. If these waves reach your ears, you hear them as a loud, dull, thunderlike thud called a sonic boom.

Reflections and Echoes

Light waves that hit a hard, smooth surface bounce off it and travel away again. This is known as reflection. We see it happening when we look in a mirror. Sound waves also bounce, or reflect, off hard, smooth surfaces. The reflected sounds may be heard after the original sound as a repeat, or echo, of the original sound.

Sound waves, however, tend to spread out and fade as they pass through air. They also lose energy as they bounce off surfaces. So echoes are fainter than the original sound. Also, unless the reflecting surface is very smooth, it bounces the sound waves in many different directions, so the returning echo is much less clear than the original sound.

Useful echoes

Sound reflection is used in underwater echo-sounding, or sonar (SOund Navigation And Ranging). Powerful, high-pitched sounds are sent through the water. When the sounds hit objects, the echoes bounce back to underwater microphones. A computer then uses the echoes to determine the distance and position of the object reflecting them. Sonar is used to measure the water's depth, map the seafloor, and find large objects such as shipwrecks, schools of fish, whales, and submarines.

Echo, echo, echo

Echoes are most obvious with loud, short, sharp sounds that bounce off large, smooth, hard surfaces such as walls, buildings, or cliffs. The average speed of sound in air is about 1,115 feet (340 m) per second. If a person made a loud handclap, and there was a wall 280 feet (85 m) away, the sound waves of the clap would take about 0.25 second to reach the wall. After bouncing off the wall, the sound waves would take the same time to travel back to the person.

So the time between the clap and its echo would be 0.5 seconds. If the reflecting surface is less than about 50 feet (15 m) away, the echo comes back too fast for us to hear it as separate from the original sound. In this situation, the echo just seems to add to the original sound and make it longer. This effect is termed reverberation. It is used in making and recording music.

Everyday echoes

We hear many echoes in daily life. But they usually happen within fractions of seconds of the original sound. They also get confused with other sounds happening at the same time. An echo is most obvious in large indoor spaces with hard walls, floors, and ceilings, such as big classrooms, gymnasiums, shopping centers, and churches. The echoes are easiest to hear when these places are almost empty and quiet. At busy, noisy times, there are so many echoes that they get mixed together and become hard to hear clearly.

Plenty of echo

Large, enclosed spaces with hard surfaces, such as shopping centers, produce a lot of echoes. These echoes are most noticeable when it is fairly quiet, so the weak echoes can be heard more clearly.

Wanted and unwanted echoes

Places such as movie theaters, concert halls, and nightclubs need to reduce and control echoes. Otherwise the audience would hear unclear, mixed-up sounds and echoes. They might use movable panels that can be adjusted to suit different sounds. Or they use curtains of special sound-absorbing material, However, certain kinds of singing and music sound better with echoes. In a large building, such as a church or temple with plenty of echoes, singer can sound far away and lonely. To some people this sound can be very moving.

How We Hear Sounds

The ear is an amazing sense organ. It is able to hear a huge range of volumes and frequencies of sound. The ear changes sounds into patterns of tiny electrical pulses called nerve signals. These nerve signals travel along the auditory nerve to the brain. In the brain, the nerve signals are analyzed and compared with patterns of signals in the memory. This enables the brain to identify the sound. In other words, the ears detect sounds, but it is the brain that analyzes and identifies them.

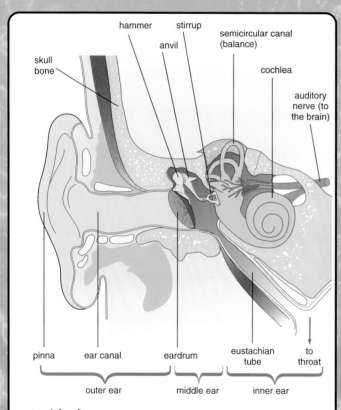

Inside the ear

Sound waves make the eardrum vibrate. This causes the row of three small bones to vibrate too. These vibrations create pressure ripples inside the fluid-filled cochlea. The cochlea changes the movement of the fluid into nerve signals.

Outer and middle ear

All the parts of the ear work together to enable us to hear. The flap on the side of the head, called the pinna, funnels sound waves traveling through the air into the outer ear canal. The ear canal is a short tube in the side of the head. It is slightly *S* shaped and measures about 0.8 to 1.2 inch (2 to 3 cm) long. The sound waves pass along the ear canal and hit the eardrum, which is a small, flexible flap of skinlike material stretched across the end of the ear canal. The eardrum is about the size of the nail on a person's little finger. Sound waves hitting the eardrum cause it to vibrate.

On the other side of the eardrum is an air-filled chamber, called the middle ear cavity. It contains three tiny ossicles, or bones, called the hammer (malleus), anvil (incus), and stirrup (stapes). These are the smallest bones in the body. The hammer is attached to the inner surface of the eardrum. As the eardrum vibrates, it passes the vibrations to the hammer, and on to the anvil and stirrup. These bones work like tiny levers to make the vibrations larger. Larger vibrations are easier to detect by the delicate parts of the inner ear.

Inner ear

The stirrup bone is attached to another flexible sheet or membrane, called the oval window. The oval window is set into the wall of the cochlea, a snail-shaped, fluid-filled organ in the inner ear. The stirrup vibrates the oval window, and the vibrations pass into the cochlea, causing ripples in its fluid. Inside the cochlea is a spiral-shaped membrane called the basilar membrane. It has 15,000 to 20,000 microscopic hair cells. Each hair cell has between 40 and 100 even tinier hairs called cilia that stick out from its upper surface. The ripples in the fluid make the cilia move. This makes the hair cells produce nerve signals. The signals pass to the auditory nerve, which takes the signals to the brain.

What we hear

The human ear can detect pitches, or frequencies, from about 20 hertz, such as the boom of thunder, to 20,000 hertz, the high-pitched sound of bird song. However, the range of hearing varies from person to person. Some people cannot detect sounds below 30 hertz. Our ability to hear high frequencies fades with age, usually starting at about 25 years old. Some older people cannot hear frequencies above about 8000 hertz.

Deep inside the ear, the tiny hairs called cilia are arranged in bunches inside the cochlea.

Hearing in Daily Life

The human ear picks up patterns of sound waves, changes them into patterns of nerve signals, and sends these signals to the brain. However, the sound waves that travel through the air are changed as we hear them. Some of these changes happen in the ear itself, and others happen in the brain. As we grow up through childhood, our brain learns to filter and adjust what our ears hear.

Always listening

The brain probably analyzes and interprets all sounds heard by the ears—even as we sleep. The mind ignores many sounds and background noises unless they become important. When you hear your name mentioned by people talking nearby, you tend to pay more attention to what they are saying. Your brain has been paying some attention to the conversation but mostly ignoring it, until it picked up sounds that were important to you.

Not quite asleep
Even during sleep, our brain keeps track of sounds and makes us wake up if there is a unfamiliar noise.

Direction of sound

Having an ear on each side of the head is much more useful than having just one ear. It allows you to hear in stereo (stereophonic), or two-ear, sound. This means you can tell the direction that a sound comes from—from the left, the right, or in between. The ears and brain figure out direction in several ways. Because the speed of sound waves in air is fairly slow (a million times slower than light rays), sound coming from the left side reaches the left ear slightly before it reaches the right ear. The time difference is less than 0.001 (one one-thousandth) of a second. But the ears and brain work so fast that they can pick up this difference. That is how you know that the sound is coming from the left side.

There are extra clues, too. Because the sound waves pass straight into the left ear, the sound is louder and clearer on that side compared to the right side. If you want to know more about the sound, you turn your head to face it. The sound waves then reach each ear at the same time, so the clarity improves in the ear that was facing away from the sound.

Too-loud sounds

The ear bones, or ossicles, in the middle ear are joined to each other. They also have tiny muscles attached to them. If the ear is exposed to loud sounds, above about 80 decibels, these muscles tighten, or tense, especially the stapedius muscle that is attached to the stirrup bone. The muscles prevent the bones from vibrating so freely. Their reduced movements mean they pass smaller vibrations into the cochlea. In this way, they prevent the cochlea from being damaged by vibrations that are too large (see page 11).

After we have been listening to very loud sounds, we might have trouble hearing sounds at normal volume, such as people talking. This effect lasts until the muscles slowly relax, so the ear bones can move freely again. However, this sound muffling system cannot deal with long exposure to loud sounds. High-frequency sounds that are also above 90 to 95 decibels in volume are especially dangerous. These sounds may damage our hearing permanently.

Artificial Sound Detection

We hear some of the sounds around us, but not all of them. The human ear has limits. It cannot pick up sound waves with very low or high frequencies, or sounds that have an intensity or volume below about ten decibels. These sound waves may reach our ears, but we cannot hear them. However, people make various machines that can create and pick up such sounds, and they use them in many different ways.

Ultrasound

Sound waves with frequencies above the average limit of human hearing, generally about 20,000 hertz, are known as ultrasonic. Our ears cannot pick them up, but various kinds of microphones and electronic machines can. So can many animals, such as horses, dogs, shrews, and bats. These animals use ultrasound to communicate, find their way, and catch prey People use ultrasound, too, in many ways.

Compared to low-frequency sounds, sounds with very high frequencies tend to spread less from their source. They stay closer together as a narrow burst, rather like the narrow light beam from a spotlight. This is one reason why ships and submarines use focused bursts of ultrasound for their sonar systems.

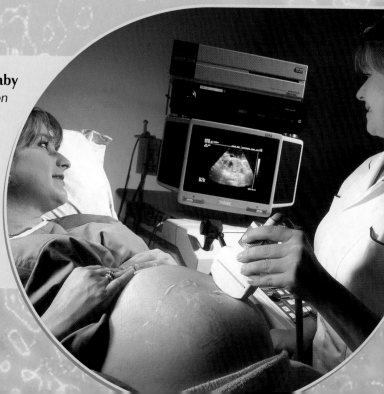

Seeing the unborn baby
In an ultrasound scan on a pregnant woman, the sounds are sent out by an emitter and received by a microphone. Both are inside the probe that the operator moves over the mother's abdomen.

24

Baby scans

The same principle—sending out very high-pitched sounds and detecting and analyzing the echoes—is used in medical ultrasound scans, which use ultrasound to create images of the inside of the body. The ultrasound is not converted into lower sound frequencies that we can hear, but changed by a computer into pictures on a screen. Such scans are given to pregnant women, to check that the baby is developing normally in the womb.

Similar, but more powerful, ultrasound scanners are used in industry to check parts and materials for stress, strain, and unseen cracks and breaks. Ultrasound even may be used for cleaning clothes! Scientists are experimenting with ultrasonic washing machines. The sound waves travel through the water, and the tiny, powerful ripples they cause can quickly shake the dirt off the clothing. This saves water, soap, and energy, compared to ordinary washing machines.

Shattering sounds

In some people, tiny hard lumps form inside the body, especially in the kidneys, gall bladder, and urinary bladder. These hard lumps are called stones, and they can cause great pain. A narrow burst of concentrated ultrasound can be directed into the body. This sound burst has enough energy to make the stones vibrate and shatter into tiny pieces. The tiny pieces then pass harmlessly out of the body.

Infrasound

Sound waves with frequencies below the average limit of human hearing, generally about 20 hertz, are known as infrasonic. They tend to spread out quickly and widely compared to ultrasound. For this reason, they are of little use for techniques such as sonar, when trying to pinpoint direction. However, infrasound waves are useful in other ways. Machinery such as engines and motors tend to make infrasonic waves. If an engine becomes worn or is out of adjustment, these waves change in pattern. Although people cannot hear infrasound, special microphones can pick it up. Electronic equipment then displays the information on a screen. The resulting pattern of infrasound can warn engineers of a breakdown before it happens.

Microphones

A microphone is a device that changes patterns of sound waves into matching patterns of tiny electrical signals— just as the ear does. Microphones come in several basic designs. Each has its own advantages and is used for certain purposes. Some are tiny, lightweight, tough, and cheap to make, like those in the mouthpiece of a cell phone, in the headsets worn by pilots, and in the microphones used to bug rooms. Other microphones are larger, heavier, more expensive, and more easily broken, but they pick up sounds much more clearly. These are used in radio and television studios and for recording music.

The small, lightweight microphone in a cell phone responds to a narrow range of frequencies, mainly those of the voice.

Sound to electricity

Once the sound waves have been turned into electrical signals, the signals can then be strengthened, or amplified, combined with others, changed in many ways, and recorded for playback later. Microphones have many everyday uses that we sometimes do not notice. They are used, for example, in telephones and security phones that allow a person to hear who is outside a door without opening it.

Simple but limited

Most types of microphones have a diaphragm—usually a very thin, flexible plastic sheet. Just like the eardrum, it vibrates when sound waves hit it. In a carbon button type of microphone, used in some cell phones, the diaphragm forms one side of a button-shaped capsule containing powderlike particles of carbon. Electricity passes through the powder, but not very easily. As the diaphragm vibrates from sound waves, it presses the particles closer together. This helps them carry electricity more easily. The result is a pattern of electrical signals through the capsule that copies the pattern of sound waves.

Other kinds of microphones

A crystal microphone is similar to the carbon button type. But it has a crystal of a mineral substance rather than a container of carbon powder. A condenser microphone uses two metal plates that are very close together. One of the plates is attached to the diaphragm. As sound waves vibrate the diaphragm, the gap between the two plates changes, and varies the electrical flow between them. A moving-coil microphone works in the opposite way of the loudspeaker described on page 40.

Shapes of sounds

Some microphones operate only in certain directions. This cuts out unwanted sounds from elsewhere.

- A bi-directional microphone picks up sounds from the sides best. This is useful when two singers use one microphone.
- A cardioid microphone picks up sound waves from in front and slightly from the sides. This is used for a group of singers.
- A hypercardioid microphone picks up sounds only from a narrow area in front. It is used for one performer.

Musical microphone
The larger microphones used in musical performances respond to many frequencies. They can be used for voice or acoustic instruments.

Animals Hear Sounds

Humans are not the only creatures that have sound-detecting organs. Not all of these creatures have ears, but they can pick up sound-based information from their surroundings. Mammals' ears are similar to ours on the inside. But the shape of the outer ear flap, or pinna, varies greatly.

Animal ears

An elephant's ear flaps are huge. They serve mainly to help keep the elephant cool, rather than to gather sound waves. Zebras and rabbits need to have good hearing to be alerted to predators. As a result, their ears are large to collect the weak waves of faint sounds. These animals can also tilt and twist their ears to face the direction from which the sounds are loudest. This ability allows them to build up a sound picture of different noises coming from different directions all around them, without moving the head or while looking away from the source of the sound. Birds' ears are also similar to our own, but they lack outer flaps and are hidden under their feathers.

Listening with care
Zebras flick their large ears back and forth to pick up the sounds of danger, such as a lion rustling in the long grass nearby.

Finding the way by sound

Some of the biggest ears, as compared to body size, belong to bats. These flying mammals use sound as other animals use sight—to find their way around and locate food. Bats use a system called echolocation, which is similar to sonar. Bats emit high-pitched clicks and squeaks, mostly ultrasonic, in a narrow burst. The sounds bounce off surrounding objects. The bat's huge ears pick up the echoes, and its brain makes sense of them to identify objects around it.

During ordinary flight, a bat produces from five to twenty sound pulses per second. As it approaches its prey, this rate rises to more than 200 pulses per second. Each pulse sweeps from high to low frequency. With such amazing echolocation, a bat can sense items as small as a tiny insect, or as thin as a human hair. It can do this even in complete darkness, when it cannot see at all. In water, dolphins and some whales use a similar system of echolocation.

No ears and odd ears

Many reptiles, such as lizards, have ears like ours, but with no outer ear flap or ear canal. The eardrum is usually visible as a round or oval shape just behind the eye. Some insects, such as grasshoppers and crickets, have similar flexible, skinlike sheets that vibrate when sounds hit them. But these hearing organs are not on the head. They are on the legs, near the knee joint.

Killing sounds

Some ocean predators, such as dolphins and killer whales, can produce powerful bursts of sound. These bursts have so much energy that they can kill or stun prey. The intensity of sound from a huge sperm whale can be more than 200 decibels. This is louder than a rocket taking off.

Did you know?

Forty percent of the large, green insects called preying mantises have absolutely no ears! Those that do have only one teardrop-shaped ear, on the underside of their body.

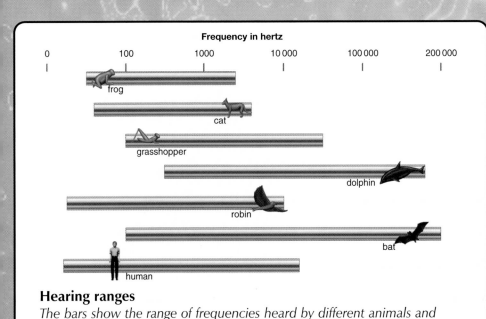

Hearing ranges
The bars show the range of frequencies heard by different animals and humans, in hertz (vibrations per second).

Producing Sounds

Probably the sounds we listen to most are the sounds of the human voice. These sounds come from the voice box, or larynx, which is in the neck. We use our voice boxes to form sounds as we talk, shout, and sing. Speech is the main way we communicate directly, face to face, with others. The voice box also produces vocalizations, which are wordless sounds such as laughter, crying, grunts, and moans. Such vocalizations are very important in daily life. Often they communicate more about our moods and emotions than words could.

Ha-ha-ha!
Laughter is not words, but it is vocalization and communicates an important meaning.

The voice box

The voice box is in the front of the neck. It lies between the lower throat above it and the windpipe, or trachea, leading to the lungs below. The outer casing of the voice box is formed from curved plates of cartilage—a tough, light, slightly flexible substance. The main airway from the nose and mouth down to the lungs passes through the voice box. Inside the lower voice box, two flaps or strips stick out from its walls, like shelves. These are the vocal folds, or vocal cords. During normal breathing, the vocal folds are apart at the rear but almost touching at the front. They form a triangle-shaped gap called the glottis. Air passes easily and silently through the glottis, into and out of the lungs.

Vocal sounds

To speak or vocalize, muscles in the voice box wall pull the vocal folds together. This action reduces the triangle-shaped gap of the glottis to a long, narrow slit (illustrated on page 33). Air passing through this slit makes the edges of the folds shake back and forth, or vibrate. This produces the voice. For louder speech, the air passes more forcefully and makes the vocal folds vibrate more. To raise the voice's pitch, or frequency, the folds are stretched tighter by muscles pulling on the cartilage around them, so they vibrate faster. Men have thicker, slower-vibrating vocal cords. Men's are about 0.8 inch (21 mm) long, compared to about 0.7 inch (17 mm) in women. This means that the average male voice is deeper.

Vocal extras

The sounds made by the vocal cords are surprisingly quiet and flat. However, the sound waves are changed on their way out. First, they pass up through the throat with the breathed-out air. Then they enter the chambers of mouth and nose. From the nose, they go through passages into the air chambers inside the facial bones, called the nasal sinuses. All these parts change the sounds and make them louder. We change the positions of the lips, tongue, cheeks, and lower jaw to change the sound waves further. As a result, each person has a voiceprint—a quality of voice and way of speaking as unique as a fingerprint.

"That doesn't sound like me"

Many people are surprised by the sound of their recorded voice. When we speak, we hear the sound waves created, as other people do. But our inner ear also responds to vibrations from the voice box that travel up through the bones and flesh of our head. This changes what the ear picks up, in a way that only we can hear. The voice on the recording is how other people hear us.

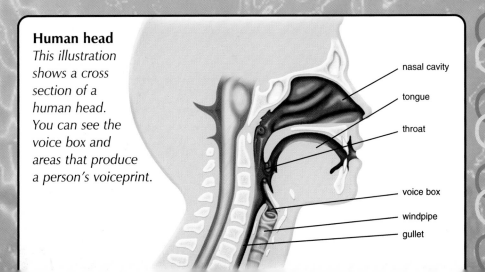

Human head
This illustration shows a cross section of a human head. You can see the voice box and areas that produce a person's voiceprint.

nasal cavity

tongue

throat

voice box

windpipe

gullet

Nature's Sound Makers

Imagine the sounds you can hear in the peace and quiet of the countryside. Nature is not always quiet. The wind rustles the grass. Birds sing and flap overhead. In summer, bees buzz lazily. Then a storm blows up, hail patters down, and thunder booms. As the storm passes, a nearby stream tinkles gently. Even at the South Pole there would still be sounds, such as the wind howling and snow crunching as it slid down a slope. In a rain forest at dawn, your ears might ring with whooping monkeys, squawking parrots, and a wide variety of other animal sounds. And when the rain comes, its hammering on the leaves would be almost deafening.

Love songs in the sea

Water carries sounds farther than air does. The songs of some whales, such as the humpback, can travel more than 120 miles (200 km) through the ocean. The male humpback sings a long, complicated song for hours, probably to attract a female. But if he was on land and sang into air, his song would travel only 3 miles (5 km).

Whale messages

The male humpback often sings while suspended deep below the surface. He has one of the loudest and longest of all whale songs, made up of clicks, grunts, moans, and wails.

Wind and water

Natural sounds fall into two main groups—weather and animals. The two main weather sound makers are wind and water. A strong wind rustles leaves and grass by shaking them against each other. The sound of wind in our ears is made by the air rushing and swirling past our outer ear flaps, making them move and vibrate. Water can also be noisy, especially when it hits something. The roar of some waterfalls can be heard 3 miles (5 km) away. As a big wave breaks on the seashore, it crashes onto itself with a giant splash that can be higher than 100 decibels. Along some rocky coasts, waves slapping into a hollow gully in the rocks make a sound like a huge hand clap. Such sounds have been known to burst people's eardrums.

Bird songs

Animals use sounds to send messages. Birds sing at dawn to tell other birds to stay out of their territories or to attract a mate. Birds are among the noisiest creatures. They make their sounds with a body part called the syrinx. This is similar in some ways to our own larynx. It contains vibrating flaps called tympanic membranes. Unlike our larynx, the syrinx is shaped like an upside-down V and lies at the base of the windpipe. It splits into two main airways, one going to each lung.

Animal calls

Birds and other animals have calls as well as songs. Calls are shorter, simpler, and less tuneful than songs. Barks, yelps, squawks, snarls, and hisses may warn of danger or tell others to keep away. Indeed, the hiss is used by many animals, such as snakes, lizards, toads, owls, and cats. In all cases it means the same: "Stay away!"

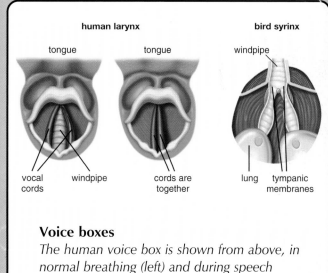

human larynx   bird syrinx

tongue   tongue   windpipe

vocal cords   windpipe   cords are together   lung   tympanic membranes

Voice boxes
The human voice box is shown from above, in normal breathing (left) and during speech (center). The bird's syrinx is similar.

Sound and Music

Musical sounds are pleasing to our ears. However, opinions often differ on what is pleasant. Musical sounds can also be described in terms of sound waves. The waves of musical sounds are usually smooth and regular, rather than jagged. Furthermore, the frequencies of the waves are linked to each other in specific ways. For example, the musical note middle C has a frequency of 256 hertz. The note at double this frequency, 512 hertz, is known as high C, or C1. Many people hear it as the same note but twice as high.

In musical terms, C1 is one octave above middle C. Other notes lie between the two, each increasing in frequency by a certain number of vibrations per second. They make up our standard musical scale: C, D, E, F, G, A, B and C1. We sing these as do, re, mi, fa, sol, la, ti, do.

Musical scales

Different musical scales are popular in different parts of the world.

- The standard Western system is the diatonic scale, with eight notes in one octave. This is the scale played with the white keys on a piano when starting from C.
- The chromatic scale has twelve notes. This is the scale played with the white and black piano keys.
- The pentatonic scale, used in some regions, has five notes. This is the scale played with the black piano keys.

Instruments

Musical instruments produce sounds by vibrating and creating sound waves in the air around them. On a guitar, the vibrating parts are the strings. Most instruments also make sounds in other parts. The guitar's soundboard, or body, responds to the sound waves and vibrations from the strings. It also vibrates and produces sound waves. In a saxophone, the sound source is a small vibrating strip, or reed, in the mouthpiece. The sound waves it makes are quiet, but they make the air inside the saxophone vibrate, and so the saxophone's body vibrates, too. This gives off more waves, to create the typical sound of the instrument. An important feature of a musical instrument is resonance. Resonance is explained on page 37.

Variable pitch
In stringed instruments such as the veena (similar to a sitar), the string can be pressed at preset lengths for the main notes, or stretched tighter for variable in-between pitches.

Breathing, hitting, plucking

Musical instruments are traditionally grouped according to how the sounds are produced. The sound of a wind instrument, such as a flute, recorder, panpipe, or penny whistle, is made by blowing air into it. Reed instruments, such as the oboe, bassoon, clarinet, and saxophone, have one or two vibrating reeds. In brass instruments, such as the trumpet, French horn, tuba, and trombone, the player's lips work like a reed to vibrate and make a buzzing noise that passes into the air chamber inside. Percussion instruments are hit, banged, shaken, or scraped. They include drums and cymbals. String instruments, such as the guitar and harp, have stretched strings that vibrate when picked or plucked.

In all these instruments, different notes are made by changing the length, tension, or size of the vibrating part. A tighter string or drum head, or a smaller air space all produce higher pitch.

Strings and keyboards

A keyboard instrument, such as the piano, is played by pressing keys. Each key is connected to a different string that vibrates when hit. In this case, the frequency of the note played is preset, depending on the length and tension of the strings inside the instrument casing.

Qualities of Sound

Most of the accounts of sound waves in this book describe a single frequency of sound—that is, one sound wave. In daily life, we rarely hear single frequencies, or pure tones. Pure tones may come from electronic equipment as a very clean-sounding hum. Such a sound is sometimes heard when tuning televisions or radios. Most of the sounds we hear, though, are a combination of frequencies. The number of different frequencies in a sound, the relationships of these frequencies to each other, and their intensities or volumes relative to each other, hugely affect the overall quality of the sound.

Too fast
A guitar string's vibrations are too fast for the eye to see but can be captured by a high-speed camera.

Fundamentals and harmonics

Imagine a plucked guitar string vibrating. The whole string bends back and forth along its length, like a bow. It moves most in the middle of the string. It sends sound waves into the air, which give a certain pitch, or note, at this frequency. This is called the fundamental frequency, or first harmonic.

But real guitar strings, rather than imagined ones, rarely do this. They vibrate in a more complicated way. Combined with the fundamental vibrations are half-length vibrations. In these, the string bends or bows in two parts, with a point of stillness in the middle. The frequency, or note, produced by these vibrations is called the second harmonic. There is also a third harmonic, and so on. All these vibrations happen at the same time and affect each other, adding yet more harmonics. It all happens too fast to see. But the result is that the string produces a mixture of sound frequencies, rather than one single frequency. The fundamental frequency is usually the loudest. The others add an extra quality that in musical instruments is called timbre.

Vibrating objects

The vibration of the guitar string may seem complicated enough already, but there is more! The sound waves it produces travel and hit the body of the guitar. On an acoustic guitar, the sound waves bounce around inside the body's hollow interior. The body of an acoustic guitar is usually made of thin sheets of springy wood. As sound waves hit them, the sheets take up the wave energy and start to vibrate.

Resonance

Each part of the guitar body, like any object, has a frequency, called its resonant frequency, at which it naturally vibrates best. Incoming sound waves make different parts of the body resonate at their own resonant frequencies—and this sends out yet more sound waves into the surrounding air. The overall result is a complex combination of sound waves from both the string and the body parts of the guitar. This gives the full sound of an acoustic guitar. Other musical instruments work similarly. They produce notes that are combinations of fundamentals, harmonics, and resonant frequencies. This is how we can identify the same musical note played on a guitar, a piano, a trumpet, or any other instrument.

Smashing

Most objects have their own resonance —the frequency at which they vibrate most effectively. If sound waves of this frequency hit an object, they make it vibrate, or resonate. This can be spectacular. If a very loud sound strikes a fragile object such as a wine glass that matches the glass's resonant frequency, the glass absorbs the energy and vibrates more and more until it shatters.

Exploded by sound
A wine glass exposed to sound waves at its own resonant pitch will vibrate more and more until it breaks apart.

Sound and Noise

Noise is sound that is unpleasant, irritating, or unwanted. It is all around us most of the time, for example, traffic noise in the street, chatter in the classroom, machines in factories and workshops, and the roar of planes and home appliances such as washing machines and vacuum cleaners. The sound waves of noise differ from the sound waves of music. Noise sound waves are usually jagged, with a random mixture of frequencies and volumes. Music, on the other hand, has smooth, regular sound waves.

Problems with noise

In most everyday situations, noise can be controlled or reduced in some way. If an appliance, such as a washing machine in the next room, is making a loud noise, we can close the door to the room to prevent the sound waves from coming through. Some of the sound waves are absorbed. Others reflect off the door back into the room with the appliance, bounce around, and gradually fade in energy. With the door closed, the sound is louder in the room where the appliance is and quieter in the other room.

Much of the science of acoustics is aimed at controlling or reducing noise—for example, lessening the sound of motors and engines for people inside trains, planes, and vehicles, reducing the noise of planes for people living near airports and eliminating external noise in recording studios.

Controlling sound and noise

Controlling sound is very important in music clubs and concert halls. At a typical music event, only about one tenth of the sound heard by the audience comes directly through the air from the performers, instruments, and loudspeakers. The rest is reflected off the ceiling, floor, walls, and other surfaces. This is particularly true of deep, or low-frequency, sounds. These may be reflected twenty or more times before they are heard. High-frequency sounds behave differently. They tend to lose energy faster each time they are reflected.

Big and deep
Large organs have huge pipes for very deep notes. They reverberate, or echo, for many seconds.

Reverberation

Acoustic engineers help architects and designers produce places where sounds and music can be heard most clearly. This is why many performance halls have large panels of special materials in the ceiling or around the stage. Some materials absorb unwanted sounds, while others reflect wanted sounds out to the audience.

One important feature of music hall design is reverberation. Reverberation is the time it takes for all the echoes of a sound to die away, after the sound itself has stopped. In a place with hard surfaces, such as a church or gymnasium, reverberation times may be several seconds. A certain amount of reverberation makes a musical sound more interesting and pleasant. However, too much reverberation makes sounds swirl around and blend so that they become unclear.

Too much reverberation

Reverberation is a problem for public address announcers in such places as train and bus stations, airports, and stadiums. In a large, enclosed area with hard surfaces, the echoes of one word reverberate as the next word begins. This makes speech hard to understand. Announcers learn to talk slowly to allow reverberation to fade. It helps if listeners partly block their ears, cutting out the weaker reverberating echoes.

Managing Sound

A loudspeaker is not always loud, but it changes patterns of electrical signals into sound waves. In this sense, the way it works is the opposite of the moving-coil microphone described on page 27. A basic public address system has a microphone to turn the sound waves into electrical signals, an amplifier to make these signals stronger, various controls to adjust volume and frequencies (low, or bass, and high, or treble), and a loudspeaker to turn the electrical signals back into sound. There are usually at least two loudspeakers to create the stereophonic, or two-ear, sound. This gives the effect of different voices, instruments, and other sound sources coming from different directions.

Sound power

The sound produced by a system is usually measured in watts of electrical power that are fed along the wires to the loudspeaker.

- A small home system might have 10 to 50 watts per side, or channel (left or right).
- A larger home system could have 200 watts per channel.
- A sound system in a small concert hall usually has over 1000 watts per channel.
- Huge sound systems at outdoor venues, such as sports stadiums, are measured in tens of thousands of watts.

Headphones and earphones

Headphones are small loudspeakers worn over the ears. They have cups enclosing the ears to keep out sounds from the surroundings. This allows the listener to hear only through the headphones. Earphones are even smaller versions that fit into the ears.

Basic parts

A typical loudspeaker has a cabinet or box. In this is the cone or diaphragm. The diaphragm is usually funnel shaped and made from thin cardboard or plastic. The electrical signals pass through a wire coil behind the middle of the cone. Electricity passing through a wire coil makes a magnetic field around it. Next to the coil is a very strong magnet, usually shaped like a ring. So both the coil and this magnet have

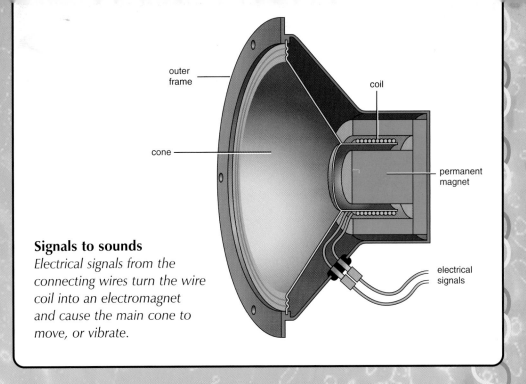

outer
frame

coil

cone

permanent
magnet

Signals to sounds
*Electrical signals from the
connecting wires turn the wire
coil into an electromagnet
and cause the main cone to
move, or vibrate.*

electrical
signals

magnetic fields. The coil's magnetic field changes as the electrical
signals change. This causes the two magnetic fields to push or pull
against each other. (This is called magnetic attraction and repulsion.)
The permanent magnet is fixed, but the coil can move. It vibrates back
and forth and vibrates the attached cone. The vibrating cone makes
sound waves that travel out of the loudspeaker.

Types of loudspeakers

Larger objects tend to vibrate more slowly than smaller ones, and so
produce lower, or deeper, sounds. High-quality loudspeakers usually
have several different-sized cones to produce the full range of
frequencies more clearly. The biggest cone, the woofer, produces low,
or bass, frequencies, such as the sounds from drums, bass guitar,
double bass, and tuba. These sounds are usually below 200 hertz. The
medium-sized cone handles the middle frequencies, such as those of
the human voice and middle notes from guitars, pianos, and trumpets.
The smallest cone, the tweeter, produces the highest frequencies,
above 2000 hertz. It makes sound waves such as the tinkle of a
triangle and the *ssss* of cymbals. Some speakers, especially for loud
modern music, have sub-woofers. Sub-woofers produce very low
frequencies, some below the range of human hearing. These very deep
sounds are not heard. Instead, the body feels them as thumps in the
chest and abdomen.

Sound Reduction

Soundproofing or sound-damping materials are designed to absorb, or soak up, the energy of sound waves. These materials are usually soft, and they bend as sound waves hit them. The energy of the sound waves is changed into the energy of motion, rather than being reflected as more sound waves. A rough surface and a spongy, honeycomb-like structure also make good soundproofing materials. The sound waves enter the material and are trapped within it. Everyday items that help absorb sounds include carpets, curtains, and other types of fabrics, especially where they cover hard, smooth surfaces such as floors and walls, which would otherwise reflect the sound waves.

Noisy noise annoys

Our moods, emotions, and general health can be hugely affected by sounds. Gentle music is calming, while harsh noise is distracting and irritating. Loud noises can also damage the ears and cause hearing problems. People who work in noisy places wear earmuffs or earplugs to protect their ears from damage and make the noise less bothersome.

Safe ears
Earmuffs protect the ears from the deafening roar of jet engines.

Soundproofing

Soundproofing materials in the form of sheets or tiles can be attached to ceilings, walls, and floors. They also can be put in the gaps between these surfaces when buildings are being built, to reduce the amount of sound that can pass through. Windows are a special problem. Windows with one pane of glass vibrate when sound waves hit it. This transmits the sound waves into the air on the other side of the window. Windows with two panes of glass help to reduce noise by absorbing the sound energy in two stages. Each pane absorbs some of the sound.

Scientists are always researching new soundproofing materials. They are especially interested in materials that can keep in warmth, too, so they can be used for both sound and heat insulation. For example, some kinds of plastic are difficult to get rid of or recycle after use. But they might be used as a raw material for insulation for both heat and sound. The plastic is heated gently to make it softer. Then it is shredded into a mass of fine, fluffy threads. These threads are tangled together to make a plastic version of cotton.

Sound and buildings

Buildings near main roads, railway lines, and airports are designed to include many kinds of soundproofing. Soundproofing materials are added to the frame, walls, floors, ceilings, windows, pipes, and ventilation, and even in furnishings such as carpets and curtains.

Soundproofing not only helps keep out noise from the outside. It also reduces sounds made inside a building by machines, fans, air-conditioning, and water in pipes. Some buildings have a main frame made of stiff beams and girders. This framework can pick up the energy of sound waves and start to vibrate. The vibration transmits the sounds to other parts of the building. Stiff pipes, such as water pipes, drainpipes, and air-conditioning ducts, can also carry sounds. To reduce this, the parts of the building frame or the pipes are joined using pads of rubber or a similar material that absorbs the vibrations.

Technology of Sound

Modern technology allows us to change and work with sounds. We can do this when sounds are in the form of real sound waves and also in the form of patterns of electrical signals. This is the basis of the recording industry for all kinds of sounds. Many of the sounds we listen to every day have been stored or recorded in some form, to be played back later. We listen to recorded music, speech, and other sounds on our home sound systems, personal stereos, radios, televisions, and computers. We listen to recorded sounds play in cars, at the movies, and in stores—almost anywhere, and often without noticing it.

Sources of sound

Most of the recorded sounds we hear are picked up by microphones that change patterns of sound waves from voices, musical instruments, and other sources into electrical signals. However, sounds can also be created as electrical signals, by equipment such as synthesizers, computers, and samplers. They begin as electricity rather than sound. These electrical signals are then fed into loudspeakers, which turn them into sound waves. A part, or sample, of an existing sound can be recorded and played backwards, cut into smaller parts and repeated, and changed using many other techniques. Modern synthesizers and similar devices can produce almost any sound we want—the only limits are in our imagination.

FX

Electrical signals representing sounds can be changed in many ways to give certain effects, or FX, when they are finally turned back into sounds. For example, an echo effect makes a copy of the sound, which is heard just after the real one, to give the impression of a real echo. The flanger effect produces a whooshing or falling sound. New effects are being invented all the time.

Mixing and EQ

The electrical signals from various sound sources are usually fed into a mixing board. This can alter the volume of any sound. Each sound, such as a person's voice, a guitar, a piano, or drums, is fed into its own channel, or track. Mixing boards have 16, 32, 64, or more channels to mix together many different sound sources.

In each channel, the mixer can change not only the volume, but also the different frequencies that make up that sound, by changing the electric signals. For example, the lower, or bass, frequencies can be increased, while the midrange and higher frequencies are reduced. This makes the sound seem deeper and more booming. The process of altering the balance of frequencies is known as equalization, or EQ. A simple type of EQ is seen in the tone controls on a home music system, which are usually labeled as bass, middle, and treble. In a mixing board, the signals are usually stored or recorded in some way—usually on magnetic tape, CD, or computer disc.

Lots of knobs
A recording engineer works at a huge mixing board in a recording studio. Every tiny piece of every sound, from voices or instruments, can be adjusted.

Too much in tune?

Modern recording equipment can even make bad singers sound in tune! The singer's voice is recorded, and for each note of the song the voice is analyzed for its frequency, or pitch. If it is different from the correct frequency, the note is automatically adjusted. However, this can make the singer's voice so exactly in tune that it sounds odd. Very slight variation in frequency is a natural part of most singing.

Sounds and Numbers

As sound waves move through the air, their strength and frequency vary in a continuous way. This happens as the air pressure smoothly changes up and down for the peaks and troughs of the waves. In the digital sound reproduction system, these smooth changes are broken up into tiny steplike changes. In the traditional system, called analog, the real sound is simply captured in its original, smoothly varying form. Imagine walking to the top of a steep hill. Going up the continuous gradual slope is the analog version. Walking up steps is the digital version: the slope is separated into a series of small, equal stages.

Analog to digital

When a microphone turns sound waves into electrical signals, these signals are analog. To make them digital, the signals are chopped up or sampled, very fast—usually 44,100 times each second (44,100 hertz). Each time, the different frequencies that make up the overall sound are measured and changed into codes made up of numbers. This can be done in great detail, since there are more than 32,000 numbers to choose from. Each time, the result is a set of numbers that captures all the frequencies and their volumes. Then the same thing is done again and again—44,100 times each second. Before the sounds are played back, they are changed back into analog electrical signals for the loudspeakers.

Back into sounds
Digitally coded sounds are changed to analog signals for the speakers.

Advantages of digital

Representing sounds as digital electrical signals, rather than analog ones, has many advantages. It allows sounds to be fed into a computer and changed and stored there because computers, too, are digitally controlled. They use digital electronic pulses to stand for everything they process. Once sounds are digitized into numbers, the computer can display them on screen, chop them up into small parts, make them louder or quieter, raise or lower their pitch, reverse them, change their speed, and just about anything else.

Recorded sound also can be copied more accurately in digital form. In digital recording, the features of the sound, such as pitch and volume, are changed into number strings that are copied as separate signals or pulses. These signals are checked by the electronic circuitry so they are exactly the same as in the original. In the analog system, small variations creep in each time copying is done, no matter how accurate the electronics. So the more times the recording is copied, the more it changes and worse the quality becomes. A digital recording can be copied many times without losing quality.

Still analog

Some people do not like the sound quality from digital formats, such as CD and DVD. They say these sounds are lifeless or too perfect. The older format of musical recording on vinyl is analog (see page 49). Some musicians and recording experts prefer the slight variations and imperfections of the analog system, which they say bring life and character to the sound.

On the decks

Disc jockeys work with vinyl discs by hand, for direct physical control of the sound.

Storing Sounds

There are several ways of storing or recording sounds. They can be kept on tapes or discs, or in electronic microchips. The amount of sound that can be stored varies a lot, too. One way of recording uses light. This is how CDs and DVDs are recorded. The sounds are turned into digital code. This is a huge list of combinations of the numbers 0 and 1. In electrical form, the 0 stands for no pulse of electricity, and the 1 means a pulse. On a CD or DVD, the 0 is a tiny smooth part of the disc, and the 1 is a microscopic pit on the disc surface. A typical CD has 3 billion of these flats and pits, in a line 3 miles (5 km) long. The line is the shape of a spiral on the shiny underside of the disc. The spiral begins near the center and curves around and around to the outer edge.

Sounds in code
The microscopic pits on a CD's underside represent sounds coded in digital form.

MP3

MP3 (MPEG layer 3) is a digital sound storage format, used for computers and over the Internet. MPEG means Moving Picture Coding Experts Group. This is a group of people set up to figure out how to digitize pictures and sounds so they would take up little computer memory. Layer 3 indicates the type of mathematical calculation used. MP3 format requires only one-twelfth of the memory needed by normal digital format.

Reading the disc

For the disc to be read (for the information from it to be changed into sound), the disc spins around as a very narrow laser beam shines on it. Where there is a pit, the laser beam is reflected. A sensor detects this and makes an electrical pulse. Where there is no pit, there is no reflection and no electrical pulse. All this happens 1.3 million times every second. Electrical circuits in the disc player receive the stream of coded pulses and change them into signals for the amplifier and loudspeakers. A typical CD stores about 74 minutes of recorded sound, using a digital memory of 740 megabytes. A DVD stores seven or eight times more than a CD, which is more than 5,000 megabytes, or 5 gigabytes. But in a movie on DVD, less than 1/100th of the information is for sounds. The rest is for the pictures.

Listen at work
Modern personal music devices, such as minidisc and MP3 players, are small enough to fit into a pocket.

Magnetic storage

On magnetic tape, the sounds are represented by microscopic patches of magnetism. These patches of magnetism are in the tape's coating, which contains iron. On small cassette-type tapes, the sounds are coded in analog form. In the format called DAT, or digital audio tape, the sounds are in digital form. In a computer, a floppy disc or hard disc also stores sounds in digital magnetic form.

Vinyl storage

On old vinyl records, sounds are stored in analog form as a groove spiraling from the edge of the disc inward. This is the opposite of the spiral on a CD. Wiggles in the groove representing sound frequencies and volumes are picked up by a needle, or stylus, on a record player. The stylus rests in the groove. As the vinyl record spins, the wiggles and waves of the groove move the sylus. These movements are changed into electrical signals.

Seeing Sounds

For most people, sight is their main sense. It brings more information into the brain than all the other senses combined. We often find it easier to understand sounds, to work with them and to change them, when they are shown in visual form. Also, our eyes can gaze quickly around a scene. Then they can study certain parts of the scene in detail by looking straight at them. Our ears cannot pick out parts of what we hear in this way. However, some people do learn to do this. They concentrate their mind on sounds of a certain pitch or quality, while trying to ignore the others. For example, musicians learn to pick out and follow the sound of their own instrument, from the overall sound of a band or orchestra. But this is all done in the brain, not in the ears.

Chladni figures

One of the first people to recognize patterns of sound was a German scientist named Ernst Chladni. He used a large, very thin, flexible circular sheet of metal, up to 6 feet (2 m) across. On this he scattered small grains, usually of sand or salt. Then he played a single continuous note from a musical instrument, such as a violin, very near the plate. The sound waves of the note hit the plate and made it vibrate in a complex way, with different frequencies in different parts of the plate. The vibrations made the grains bounce up and down and move to the areas of least vibration, where they collected in piles and rows.

Ernst Chladni (1756-1827)

Chladni is known as a founder of the science of acoustics. He did many experiments on sound. He showed that the speed of sound varies depending on what kind of gas the waves pass through. He invented two musical instruments, the euphonium and the clavicylinder.

Using this method, Chladni produced complex and beautiful patterns of grains on the plate, like flower petals or ripples on a pond. These patterns were called Chladni figures.

Sounds on screen

The modern version of Chladni's patterns can be seen on a computer screen, where patterns of sounds are converted to lines and shapes of different colors. Many computer programs do this. One common system is MIDI, Musical Instrument Digital Interface, which uses the sounds made by musical instruments for working with in digital form on computers. Sound engineers, musicians, and record producers also use chartlike diagrams on screen. These show the different frequencies that make up a sound and how loud they are. A diagram like this can be made to move or flow across the screen as the sounds play. It often helps greatly to see this frequency spectrum, as well as hear it, in order to pick up and identify problems.

On the 'scope

An oscilloscope is a device that shows electrical signals as waves on a screen. The waves can be seen moving up and down or back and forth, which is called oscillating. Oscilloscopes are used to see the electrical signals that represent sounds that may be coming from microphones, passing through amplifiers, or going out to loudspeakers.

Sound and sight
A musician hears notes from the keyboard through speakers and also sees them as charts and graphs on the computer screen.

Summary: Sounds Every Day

The science of sound, known as acoustics, can be very complicated. It involves waves, frequencies, echoes, resonance, reverberation, and soundproofing. Sound is studied and used with many kinds of electrical equipment, such as microphones, mixers, amplifiers, loudspeakers, computers, and oscilloscopes. There are various ways of recording or storing sounds, such as discs, tapes, and microchips. Sound experts talk about energy, intensity, hertz, decibels, and Mach numbers.

But we can also talk about sounds in a much simpler way. They can be low or high, quiet or loud, soft or harsh, pleasing or annoying. For many people, sounds are not technical—they are fun. People get great pleasure from making music and singing in clubs, theaters, local halls, and their own homes.

Sounds are big business. Singing stars and music groups can become very rich. Concerts, orchestras, bands, radio programs, and movie soundtracks can make million-dollar profits. A television commercial sis more likely to be successful if it has a voiceover from a famous celebrity, rather than an unknown person.

Sounds are also far more important in daily life than we often realize. Our brains store thousands and thousands of them. Like sights and smells, hearing a sound can bring memories flooding back. A certain piece of music, a powerful speech, words from a close friend, or the wail of a warning siren can change our thoughts, feelings, and emotions in a few seconds and affect our lives for years to come.

World music
Some sounds, such as the rhythmic beat of drums, are popular throughout the world.

Glossary

acoustics scientific study of sound

amplify to make larger or more powerful

amplitude height of a wave, such as a sound wave, from its middle point to the top of its peak or bottom of its trough

analog working by continuously changing or varying amounts

auditory nerve main nerve that carries signals from the ear to the brain

cochlea snail-shaped part deep in the ear that changes sound vibrations to nerve signals

decibel unit for measuring the intensity of sound, which is similar to loudness

diaphragm thin sheet that can move back and forth, or vibrate, easily, used in microphones and loudspeakers

digital working in small, separate steps or stages

disperse spread out from one place to many others

Doppler effect change in the frequency of a wave as its source moves in relation to the listener

eardrum flexible flap inside the ear that vibrates when sounds hit it

echo sound that is bounced, or reflected, and returns to be heard slightly later

echolocation finding the way and detecting objects using sound, by analyzing echoes from them

frequency how often something happens, for instance how many times a wave occurs in a certain time

fundamental in sound, the main pitch, or frequency, of several different frequencies; the one that defines the overall pitch, or note

glottis gap between the two vocal cords in the voice box

harmonic pitch, or frequency, of sound related to the main or fundamental pitch, and that produces a pleasing combination with it

hertz (Hz) unit of frequency used to measure pitch of sound (1 hertz = 1 vibration per second)

infrasonic sound in which the frequency of the sound waves is lower than can be detected by the human ear, normally below 25 to 30 hertz

insulation material that reduces the flow of heat, sound, or electricity

intensity in sound, the measure of energy in a sound wave, similar to volume

larynx voice box in the neck, where vocalizations are made

Mach unit of the speed of sound. Mach 1 is the speed of sound in a certain substance under certain conditions

magnetic field area around a magnet where the magnetism extends

ossicles tiny bones in the ear that carry sound vibrations from the eardrum to the cochlea

peak top of a wave

pinna flap on the side of the head that funnels sound waves into the ear canal

pitch highness or lowness of sound, measured as frequency

pressure amount of force pressing on a certain area

propagate to transmit energy, waves, etc.

reed strip in the mouthpiece of a musical instrument, such as a saxophone, that vibrates when the player blows into the mouthpiece

reflection sound, light, or heat bouncing back from a surface

resonance vibration of an object at its own natural rate (frequency) caused by sound

reverberation multiple reflections of sounds heard after the original sound, but not as late or distinct as an echo

sonar SOund NAvigation and Ranging, similar to echolocation

stapedius muscle attached to the stirrup bone in the middle ear

stereophonic sound detected by two ears or two microphones, so its direction can be identified

supersonic moving faster than sound

syrinx voice box of birds

timbre overall quality and features of sound that allow us to identify what made it

trachea windpipe in the throat that leads to the lungs

transmit transfer of energy from one place to another, usually as waves

transverse sideways or crossways direction, rather than lengthways or longitudinal

ultrasonic sound in which the frequency of the sound waves is higher than can be detected by the human ear, usually above 18,000 to 20,000 hertz

velocity speed in a certain direction

vocalizations sounds made by the larynx

volume loudness of a sound

wavelength length of a wave, such as a sound wave, usually measured from one peak to the next

Further Reading

Books

The Dorling Kindersley Science Encyclopedia. New York: Dorling Kindersley, 1999.

Oxlade, Chris. *Science Topics: Light and Sound.* Chicago: Heinemann Library, 1999.

Parker, Steve. *Science Fact Files: Light and Sound.* [need city]: Hodder-Wayland/Raintree-Steck Vaughn, 2000.

Parker, Steve. *Science Works: Sound.* [need city:] Macdonald Young Books/Gareth Stevens, 1997.

Read, Struan. *Groundbreakers: Alexander Graham Bell.* Chicago: Heinemann Library, 2000.

Searle, Bobbi. *Fascinating Science Projects: Sound.* New York: Franklin Watts, 2002.

Taylor, Barbara. *Focus on Science: Sound.* New York: Franklin Watts, 2003.

Index